THE **TESTING** SERIES

POLICE OFFICER
ROLE PLAY
EXERCISES

THE **TESTING** SERIES
expert advice on test preparation

how2become

Orders: Please contact How2become Ltd, Suite 2, 50 Churchill Square Business Centre, Kings Hill, Kent ME19 4YU.

You can also order via the e mail address info@how2become.co.uk.

ISBN: 9781907558986

First published 2012

Typeset for How2become Ltd by Molly Hill, Canada.

Printed in Great Britain for How2become Ltd by CMP (uk) Limited, Poole, Dorset

INTRODUCTION

Welcome to your new guide, police role play exercises. This guide has been designed to help you prepare for and pass the role play/interactive exercises that form part of the police officer assessment centre in England and Wales.

Approximately 65,000 people apply to join the police every year. But what is even more staggering is that only approximately 7,000 of those applicants will be successful. You could view this as a worrying statistic, or alternatively you could view it that you are determined to be one of the 7,000 who are successful. Armed with this insider's guide, you have certainly taken the first step to passing the police officer selection process.

The guide contains a number of sample role play scenarios which are designed to make it easier for you to prepare. Read the advice contained within this guide carefully and take notes as you progress.

You can also watch the accompanying video for this title online at the following website free of charge.

WWW.POLICEROLEPLAY.CO.UK

Go to the above website now and access the video.

It is important to point out at this early stage that the sample role play scenarios provided within this guide are entirely fictitious and are not the exact ones you will encounter during the assessment centre. However, they are excellent examples of the types of scenario you will encounter on the day and you will find them a huge help in your preparation.

Don't ever give up on your dreams; if you really want to become a police officer then you can do it. The way to approach the police officer role play/ interactive exercises is to embark on a programme of 'in-depth' preparation, and this guide will show you exactly how to do that.

The police officer selection process is not easy to pass. Your preparation must be focused in the right areas, and also be comprehensive enough to give you every chance of success.

If you need any further help with any elements of the police officer selection process, including application form help, written test and interview, then we offer a wide range of products to assist you. These are all available through our online shop www.how2become.co.uk.

We also run a 1-day intensive Police Officer Course. Details are available at the website www.PoliceCourse.co.uk.

Once again, thank you for your custom and we wish you every success in your pursuit to becoming a police officer.

Work hard, stay focused and be what you want!

Best wishes,

The how2become team

The How2become Team

THE ROLE-PLAY/ INTERACTIVE EXERCISES

During the police officer assessment centre you will have to deal with four interactive exercises or role plays as they are otherwise called. The type of situation that you will be confronted with varies greatly. However, examples of the types of exercises that have been used in the past include the following:

- A manager of a store that is inside a fictitious retail centre wants to discuss an issue with you that relates to the lack of security.

- A customer who has been shopping at a fictitious retail centre wants to talk to you about a conversation they have had with another customer.

- A school teacher who has been visiting the retail centre would like to discuss an issue with you regarding his/her pupils.

- A member of staff who works at the fictitious retail centre would like to discuss an issue with you.

The situation that you will have to deal with is irrelevant. It is how you interact with the role play actor and what you say that is important. You must be able to demonstrate the police officer core competencies during each role-play scenario. Examples of how you would achieve this include:

- Dealing with the role play actor in a sensitive and supportive manner;

- Having respect for people's views and feelings;

- Seeing issues from others' points of view;

- Ask relevant questions to clarify the situation;

- Listening to people's needs and interests;

- Respecting confidentiality where appropriate;

- Presenting an appropriate image;

- Trying to sort out customers' problems as soon as possible;

- Make reference to any supporting documentation, policies or procedures;

- Confirming that the customer is happy with your offered solution.

- Keeping customers updated on any progress that you make.

It is crucial that you learn the core competencies and are also able to demonstrate them during each exercise.

This part of the selection process will be split into two five-minute parts. The first part will consist of the preparation phase and the second part will be the actual activity phase that you'll be assessed against. I will now explain each phase in detail.

THE PREPARATION PHASE

During the five-minute preparation phase you will be provided with the actual scenario, either on a card or sheet of paper. You may also be provided with additional documentation that is relevant to the scenario that you'll be required to deal with. You will be taken to a desk or a separate room where you will have just five minutes in which to prepare for the activity phase. During the preparation phase you will be allowed to take notes and then use them during the activity phase. At the end of the activity phase you will normally be required to hand in your notes to the assessor. You will not be permitted to take any writing utensils into the activity phase.

Having personally been through this type of role play assessment I found that by learning the Welcome Pack prior to the assessment day made my life a lot easier. The preparation phase was easy, simply because I knew my role as customer services officer inside out. I knew the code of conduct, the equality policy statement, and all other relevant information that was applicable to my role. As soon as I turned over the role play scenario I knew exactly what I was required to do. Although the preparation phase is not assessable, you must still use the time wisely. This is how I recommend you use the time:

- Quickly read the scenario and any supporting information/ documentation. If you have already studied the Welcome Pack prior to assessment your life will be a lot easier.

- Once you have studied the scenario and any additional information/ documentation you should then separate relevant information from irrelevant information, just like you did during the written report writing stage. Write down brief notes as to what you think is relevant.

- You now need to cross match any relevant information from the scenario with procedures, policies and your responsibilities that are provided in the Welcome Pack. For example, if within the scenario it becomes apparent that somebody from the centre is being bullied or harassed, you will need to know, use and make reference to the equality policy statement during the activity phase of the assessment. Another example would be where a child has been reported missing. If this was the case then you would possibly wish to make use of the security guards, the tannoy system and also the CCTV cameras that are based around the centre.

- I would now recommend that you write down on your note paper a step by step approach as what you intend to do during the activity stage. An example of this may be as follows:

STEP 1

Introduce myself to the role actor and ask him/her how I can help them.

(Remember to be polite and respectful and treat the role play actor in a sensitive and supportive manner. You are being assessed against the core competency of respect for race and diversity during every role play scenario)

STEP 2

Listen to them carefully and ask relevant questions to establish the facts.
(How, When, Where, Why, Who)

STEP 3

Clarify the information received to check you have
understood exactly what has happened.

STEP 4

Provide a suitable solution to the problem or situation
and tell the role play actor what you intend to do.
(Remember to use keywords and phrases from the core competencies)

STEP 5

Check to confirm that the role play actor is happy with your solution.

Provide a final summary of what you intend to do and ask them
if there is anything else you can help them with.

*(Tell the role actor that you will take personal responsibility for solving
the problem and that you will keep them updated on progress)*

Once you have made your notes and created a plan of action you are now
ready to go through to the activity phase. Before we move on to this stage
of the role play assessment I will provide you with a further explanation
of how you may wish to approach the preparation phase using a sample
scenario.

SAMPLE ROLE-PLAY EXERCISE 1

SAMPLE ROLE-PLAY EXERCISE 1

You are the customer service manager at a fictitious retail centre. A member of your staff approaches you and tells you that she has been bullied by another member of staff. The woman is clearly upset by the situation and she wants you to take action.

HOW TO PREPARE

If you have already taken the time to study the Welcome Pack prior to attending the assessment then the first thing that will spring to your mind will be the equality policy statement. Within the statement you will find specific details about how to deal with situations of this nature and it is essential that you follow each step carefully. Remember that one of the assessable core competencies requires you to follow and refer to policies and procedures.

Using my 5 step plan the following is how I might deal with this type of situation:

STEP 1 - I would walk into the activity room and introduce myself to the role actor. I would ask them sensitively what the problem was and how I could help them. If there was a chair available in the room then I would ask them to sit down.

STEP 2 - I would listen very carefully to what they had to say and symapthise where appropriate. I would then start to establish the facts of the case asking them relevant questions such as:

- How long had the bullying been going on for?

- Who was involved and what had they been doing/saying?

- Were any other people involved?

- Have there been any witnesses to this incident?

- Had they asked the other person to stop bullying them and if so what was their reaction?

STEP 3 - I would then clarify and confirm with the role actor that I had gathered the correct facts.

STEP 4 - At this stage I would take full control of the situation and tell the role actor what I intended to do about the situation. I would make reference at this stage to the equality policy statement and I would use it as a basis for solving the problem. I would also use keywords and phrases that matched the core competencies.

STEP 5 - During the final stages of the role play activity stage I would check to confirm that the role play actor is happy with my solution. I would provide them with a final summary of what I intend to do and I would ask them if there is anything else that I would help them with. I would also confirm at this stage that I was going to take personal responsibility for resolving the problem and that I would keep them updated on progress as and when it occurred.

Once the 5 minute preparation phase is complete a buzzer will sound and you will then move to the activity stage of the assessment.

THE ACTIVITY PHASE

The activity stage will again last for 5 minutes and it is during this phase that you are required to interact with the role actor.

During the activity stage there will be an assessor in the room whose responsibility it is to assess you against the core competencies. Try to ignore them and concentrate fully on how you interact with the role actor. There may also be a third person in the room who will be there to shadow the assessor for quality assurance purposes. During the activity stage you will be assessed on what you did and how you did it. You will usually be graded from A to D with the highest score earning you an A to the weakest score earning you a D.

Obviously you want to aim for an A but don't be disheartened if you feel that you haven't done well on a particular exercise, as you can make up your grades in another. If you score a D against the core competency of respect for race and diversity then you will fail the entire assessment.

During the previous sample role play exercise (exercise 1) we focused on a complaint made by a member of staff who claimed that she was being bullied by another member of staff. Within the equality policy statement you will find suggested courses of action. The options here may suggest that the person asks the offender to stop, the problem is discussed with an appropriate person (you) or the option is available to make a formal complaint.

Below I have provided you with some suggested responses to this type of exercise followed by an explanation. Most of these can be applied to similar exercises surrounding harassment cases, although you should judge every situation separately and act according to the brief.

SAMPLE RESPONSES AND ACTIONS TO EXERCISE 1

RESPONSE

"Thank you for coming to see me today. I understand that you have a problem with another member of staff?"

EXPLANATION

During this type of response you are demonstrating a level of customer care and you are focusing on the needs of the individual. Remember to use open body language and never become confrontational, defensive or aggressive.

RESPONSE

"Would you be able to tell me exactly what has happened and how this has affected you? I will also need to ask you whose been bullying you, where it has been occurring and on how many occasions including dates and times."

EXPLANATION

Again you are focusing on the needs of the individual, which is important. Try to look and sound genuine and also use suitable facial expressions. In order to 'problem solve' you must first ask questions and gather the facts of the incident.

RESPONSE

"It must be very difficult for you to bring this matter to my attention; you are to be praised for this course of action."

EXPLANATION

During this response you are demonstrating a caring nature and you are providing a high level of service.

RESPONSE

"Have you asked him to stop or have you informed anybody else of this situation?"

and *"Are you aware of this happening to anybody else?"*

EXPLANATION

Here you are gathering the facts, which will help you provide a suitable resolution to the problem.

RESPONSE

"The company equality policy in relation to this kind of alleged behaviour is quite clear, it states XYZ. It will NOT be tolerated and I can assure you the matter will be dealt with."

EXPLANATION

During this response you are detailing the company equality policy. This demonstrates to the assessor that you are fully aware of the policies and procedures – this will gain you higher scores. You are also stating that this type of behaviour is not accepted and you are, therefore, challenging the inappropriate behaviour in line with the police officer core competencies.

RESPONSE

"Before I detail my solution to this problem I want to first of all confirm the details of the case. Please can you confirm that…."

EXPLANATION

During this response I am confirming and checking that the details I have obtained are correct.

RESPONSE

"Please be aware that you can make a formal complaint if you so wish? Your feelings and wishes are paramount during my investigation. What would you like to happen from here? Would you like to make a formal complaint against the individual concerned? "

EXPLANATION

By asking the complainant what they want to do, you are demonstrating that you are putting their needs first and you are respecting confidentiality.

RESPONSE

"Let me assure you that this matter will be dealt with as a priority but in the meantime I will place another member of staff with you so that you can work in a comfortable environment. Are you happy with this course of action?"

EXPLANATION

Here you are taking action to resolve the problem. You are also informing the person how you intend to resolve it. Finally you are checking that the person is happy with your actions.

RESPONSE

"May I thank you again for bringing this matter to my attention; I will keep you fully informed of all progress. I wish to inform you that I will be taking personal responsibility for resolving this issue. Is there anything else I can do for you?"

EXPLANATION

Finally you are demonstrating a high level of customer service and also checking if there is anything else that you can do for them. You are also taking personal responsibility for resolving the issue. It is important to tell them that you will keep them informed of the outcome of any investigation.

TOP TIPS FOR PREPARING FOR THE ROLE-PLAY EXERCISES

- Learn the core competencies that are being assessed and be able to 'act' out each one.
- A good way to practise for these exercises is to get a friend or family relative to 'role-play' the sample exercises contained within this guide.
- When practising the exercises, try to pick someone you know who will

make it difficult for you. Also, try to resolve each issue in a calm but effective manner, in line with the core competencies.

- You may wish to purchase a copy of the 'Police Role Play' DVD now available at www.how2become.co.uk.

- Use the preparation time wisely.

- Learn the pre assessment material before you go to the assessment. This will make your life much easier.

- Remain calm during every role-play. Even if the actor becomes confrontational, it is essential that you remain calm.

- If at any time during the role play activity phase the role play actor uses language that is either inappropriate (including swearing), discriminatory or uses any form of harassment then you must challenge it immediately. When challenging this kind of behaviour you must do so in an assertive manner without becoming aggressive. Always be polite and respectful at all times.

- Use effective listening skills during the role-play exercises and ask questions in order to gather the facts.

- Once you have gathered the facts of the case or situation then solve the problem.

On the following pages I have provided you with a number of sample role-play exercises. To begin with, read each exercise carefully and then take notes in the box provided detailing how you might deal with the situation. Make sure you have a copy of the core competencies to hand when making your notes. The accompanying video, which is free to watch online, will help you to get a better understanding of how to tackle role play/interactive exercises. Go there now and access the video:

WWW.POLICEROLEPLAY.CO.UK

SAMPLE ROLE-PLAY EXERCISE 2

SAMPLE ROLE-PLAY EXERCISE 2

You are the customer services officer at a fictitious retail centre. A school teacher has lost a pupil in the shopping centre and he wants to discuss the matter with you. He is very annoyed that it took him so long to find your office. He states that there were no security staff around and his pupil has now been missing for fifteen minutes.

He wants to know what you intend to do about it.

HOW TO PREPARE AND POSSIBLE ACTIONS

- To begin with, you should study the 'OPERATIONS' information about the centre. What does it say that possibly relates to the above scenario? Is there any CCTV?

- Are there any security staff that could help look for any missing persons?

- Is there a police station within the complex and can the police be used to respond to situations like this?

- Request the attendance of the police immediately.

- Make sure that you keep the teacher in the office with you so that they can provide further information to the police about the missing child.

- Try to gather information about the missing child – How old are they? What are they wearing? What is their name? Are there any distinguishing features? Where were they last seen?

- Try to reassure the teacher that everything will be ok.

- If there is the option of using a loudspeaker system in the shopping centre then this could be used to transmit a 'missing persons' message.

- Consider the option of using the centre's CCTV cameras to locate the missing person.

- Consider positioning a member of the security team at each exit to prevent anybody walking out with the child.

On the following page I have provided a sample response to this exercise. Read it before using the box on the following page to take notes on how you would deal with this situation.

SAMPLE RESPONSES AND ACTIONS TO EXERCISE 2

"Hello sir, my name is Richard and I'm the customer service manager for this centre. I understand that one of your pupils has gone missing in the centre – is that correct?" (Establish exactly what has happened).

"Firstly can I reassure you that the police have been called and they are on their way. I have also put a security guard at each exit to look out for the missing child. In the meantime I would like to take some notes from you.

Please can you give me a full description of the missing pupil please including their name?" (Make a list of the description.)

"Please can you tell me how long ago they have been missing for and where they were last seen?"

"Have you or anybody else been looking for the missing person and have you reported this to anybody else yet?"

"Is there a possibility that they might have wandered off to their favourite shop or gone somewhere else with another parent who was in the group?"

"Do you think they would understand their own name if we broadcast this over the loudspeaker system?"

"OK Sir, thank you for providing me with these details. This is what I propose to do in order to resolve the situation. To begin with I will check the CCTV cameras to see if we can locate the missing child. I will also brief all members of staff at the centre, including the security guards, of the missing child's description. I will also put out a tannoy announcement asking the missing child to go to the nearest customer services desk where a member of staff will meet them."

"In addition to this course of action I will also put the registered nurse on standby so that she can treat the child for shock if appropriate."

"In the meantime please stay here until the police arrive, as it is important you provide them with more information. Let me reassure you that we will do everything we possibly can to locate the missing person. I will be taking personal responsibility for resolving this issue and I will keep you updated on progress as and when it occurs."

NOTES FOR SAMPLE ROLE-PLAY EXERCISE 2

SAMPLE ROLE-PLAY EXERCISE 3

SAMPLE ROLE-PLAY EXERCISE 3.

You are the customer services officer at a fictitious retail centre. One of the centre store managers wants to see you about a gang of youths who are standing outside his shop behaving in an anti-social manner, swearing and obstructing customers from entering his shop. He is very annoyed at the situation and is losing money because potential customers are not allowed to shop in comfort without feeling threatened.

HOW TO PREPARE AND POSSIBLE ACTIONS

- To begin with you should study the 'OPERATIONS' information and the 'CODE OF CONDUCT' information in the Welcome Pack. What do they say that possibly relates to the above scenario? Is this kind of behaviour tolerated? Can people who behave in such a manner be escorted from the centre and should the police be involved? Can you involve the security staff or use the CCTV cameras to provide the police with evidence?

- Remember that the manager is annoyed at the situation and therefore you may have to diffuse a confrontational situation in the first instance. Remember to be firm but stay calm and never become confrontational yourself.

On the following page I have provided a sample response to this exercise. Read it before using the box on the following page to take notes on how you would deal with this situation.

SAMPLE RESPONSES AND ACTIONS TO EXERCISE 3

"Hello Sir, thank you for coming to see me today. My name is Richard and I am the customer services officer at the centre. I understand there is an issue with a gang of youths outside your shop?" (Establish the facts of the incident by asking relevant questions).

"Can I first of all say that I fully understand how frustrating this must be for you as you are losing customers all the time the problem is present. I wish to apologise unreservedly for any problems that you are experiencing at the centre. I have called the police and they are on their way. In the meantime it is important that I take into consideration your feelings and opinions. Therefore, please can you provide me with some information about what has been happening?" (Make a list of what has happened.)

"How many people are there outside your shop? Has this happened before or is this the first time?"

"Have you reported it to anyone else? Can you provide me with a description of the people who are creating the problem? What type of language are they using?"

"May I reassure you Sir that in line with the code of conduct at the centre will not tolerate any form of anti-social behaviour and we have the power to remove people from the building and prevent them from re-entering at a later point. Whilst we await the arrival of the police I will try to see if the CCTV cameras have picked up anything."

"I am sorry that you have had to go through this experience Sir but we will do everything we can to rectify the problem. As the customer services officer for the centre it is my responsibility to ensure you receive the highest standard of customer care. With that in mind I will be taking full responsibility for resolving this issue and I will keep you updated of all progress as and when it occurs. Is there anything else I can help you with?"

NOTES FOR SAMPLE ROLE-PLAY EXERCISE 3

SAMPLE ROLE-PLAY EXERCISE 4

SAMPLE ROLE-PLAY EXERCISE 4

You are the Customer Service Manager at a fictitious retail centre. A customer would like to see you about an issue surrounding a dog that is in the shopping centre. She is very annoyed that a dog has been allowed to enter the shopping centre and wants to know what you are going to do about it. The dog is an 'assistance dog' for a visually impaired customer.

HOW TO PREPARE AND POSSIBLE ACTIONS

- To begin with you should study the 'OPERATIONS' information, the 'CODE OF CONDUCT' information and the 'EQUALITY POLICY' statement relating to the centre. What do they say that possibly relates to the above scenario? Are 'assistance dogs' permitted? If the answer is 'yes' then the person may not have any grounds for complaint. However, it is important to listen to the complaint before responding in a calm but firm manner.

- Remember to be confident in your handling of the situation and refer to the policy of the centre for such issues. Do not get drawn into personal opinions but stick to the code of conduct for the centre and apply it accordingly.

On the following page I have provided a sample response to this exercise. Read it before using the box on the following page to take notes on how you would deal with this situation.

SAMPLE RESPONSES AND ACTIONS TO EXERCISE 4

"Hello Madam, my name is Richard and I am the customer services officer for the centre, thank you for coming to see me today. I understand there is an issue with a dog in the shopping centre. Please would you explain what the problem is?"

Listen to the customer's complaint and choose an appropriate moment to respond. If at any time the customer uses inappropriate or discriminatory language then you must challenge it in an appropriate manner. It is important that you ask relevant questions in order to establish the facts of the case.

"Whilst dogs are not permitted in the shopping centre, there is an exception for 'assistance dogs' like the one you have just described. Our code of conduct states that assistance dogs for the visually impaired are permitted in the centre. The centre will not discriminate against persons with disabilities and we will do everything we can to help their shopping experience to be a pleasurable one."

"We have a legal requirement to allow 'assistance dogs' into the centre and if we were to ignore these rules we would be in contravention of those laws. I am sorry Madam but in this instance I am unable to take any action. Thank you for coming to see me and have a good day."

NOTES FOR SAMPLE ROLE-PLAY EXERCISE 4

SAMPLE ROLE-PLAY EXERCISE 5

SAMPLE ROLE-PLAY EXERCISE 5

You are the Customer Service Manager at a fictitious retail centre. A disabled customer would like to see you about an issue involving the use of disabled parking spaces at the centre. She is very upset and annoyed that people who do not have a disabled parking badge are using the car parking spaces that are designated for disabled persons. She states that there are no disabled parking spaces available and she has had to park a long distance away from the shops.

HOW TO PREPARE AND POSSIBLE ACTIONS

- To begin with you should study the Westshire Centre pack in order to see what it states in relation to disabled parking spaces. You will notice that there are a number of designated spaces specifically for disabled persons.

- Be prepared for the role actor being both upset and angry. You will need to use your skills to both defuse a potentially angry customer and to resolve the matter successfully.

- With this type of incident you may need to apologise for the centre not monitoring the use of the car park. You will also need to explore the different options for resolving the issue for the current customer.

On the following page I have provided a sample response to this exercise. Read it before using the box on the following page to take notes on how you would deal with this situation.

SAMPLE RESPONSES AND ACTIONS TO EXERCISE 5

"Hello Madam, my name is Richard and I am the customer services officer for the centre, thank you for coming to see me today. I understand there is an issue with the incorrect use of the disabled parking spaces? Please would you explain what the problem is?"

Listen to the customer's complaint and choose an appropriate moment to respond. If at any time the customer uses inappropriate or discriminatory language then you must challenge it in an appropriate manner. It is important that you ask relevant questions in order to establish the facts of the case. It is likely that the centre is at fault in a situation like this for failing to monitor and control the use of the disabled parking spaces. If this is the case then you must apologise.

"I fully sympathise with your situation here and want to apologise unreservedly for not monitoring the use of the disabled car parking spaces. I would like to resolve this issue for you. To begin with I would like to ask you a few questions which will help me to gather sufficient information in order to get to the root of the problem. Can you tell me whereabouts exactly have you witnessed the misuse of the disabled car park spaces and is this the first time it has occurred?"

It is important that you gather sufficient information from the customer. This will give you enough information in order to resolve the issue satisfactorily. However, remember that you only have five minutes in which to complete the role play exercise. Whilst the role play actor is speaking, demonstrate effective listening skills and have an open stance. This will include nodding your head and using effective listening skills to show that you are meeting the core competency of effective communication.

"Now that I have gathered sufficient information I will try to resolve the issue to your satisfaction. First of all I can assure you that I will put in place suitable car park patrols to prevent this from happening again. I would also like to provide you with my contact telephone number so that you can contact me directly if you attend the shopping centre in the future and you are unable to find a suitable disabled parking space. If you need to contact me I will immediately arrange for a member of staff to locate a suitable parking space for you which is close to the centre. I will take full responsibility for ensuring this issue does not occur again. Is my resolution to your satisfaction?"

I believe it is important to say the words "I will take full responsibility" during the role play scenario. Using this phrase will demonstrate to the assessor that you are meeting the core competency of personal responsibility.

NOTES FOR SAMPLE ROLE-PLAY EXERCISE 5

SAMPLE ROLE-PLAY EXERCISE 6

SAMPLE ROLE-PLAY EXERCISE 6

You are the Customer Service Manager at a fictitious retail centre. A mother wants to see you immediately. The mother is crying and appears to be in shock. The mother informs you that her child, a six year old boy, has collapsed in the shopping mall just outside the management centre. She informs you that a member of the public is giving him first aid as you speak, but she wants you to raise the alarm and get professional help immediately.

HOW TO PREPARE AND POSSIBLE ACTIONS

- With incidents of this nature you will need to act very quickly and prioritise your actions. The main priority is to get help for the boy. As soon as you are aware that the boy has collapsed you must do the following:

    1. Dial 999 and call for an ambulance.

    2. Inform the medical centre so that the nurse can attend.

- Be prepared for the role actor being extremely upset. Once you have raised the alarm you will need to gather as much information as possible in order to deal with the incident. Time is of the essence but you must remember to remain calm and in control.

On the following page I have provided a sample response to this exercise. Read it before using the box on the following page to take notes on how you would deal with this situation.

SAMPLE RESPONSES AND ACTIONS TO EXERCISE 6

"Hello Madam, my name is Richard and I am the customer services officer for the centre, thank you for coming to see me today. Please would you explain what the problem is?"

Let the customer speak and listen intently. As soon as you become aware that the child has collapsed ask the mother to provide the following information:

1. The exact location of the incident.

2. The age and gender of the child.

"Please can you confirm the exact location of your son and also tell me his age?"

As soon as you have this information and you have verified that it is correct, inform the mother that you will raise the alarm immediately by calling for an ambulance and also contacting the medical centre.

"OK madam thank you for the information. I will immediately call 999 and arrange for the ambulance to attend. I will also contact the medical centre and request that the nurse attends the scene immediately. I fully appreciate how distressed you must be but I assure you I will take full responsibility for dealing with this incident."

I recommend that you make provision for dialling 999 yourself so that you are 100% certain the ambulance is on its way. When you contact the emergency services and the medical centre you will need to pass on as much information as possible about the child and his injuries. You may also decide to arrange for a security guard to meet the ambulance crew when they arrive at the scene so that they can guide them to the exact location of the incident. You should also consider that the mother is in shock and she too will require medical attention. This information will need to be relayed to the ambulance crew.

You may also decide to use the tannoy system to request that all medically trained staff make their way to the management office so that they are all in one controlled location.

Once you have raised the alarm and arranged for immediate care to the scene of the incident you will need to look after the mother who is in shock.

This type of scenario is designed to assess your ability to remain calm and in control, whilst having the ability to act quickly and decisively.

**POLICE OFFICER
ROLE PLAY EXERCISES**

NOTES FOR SAMPLE ROLE-PLAY EXERCISE 6

SAMPLE ROLE-PLAY EXERCISE 7

SAMPLE ROLE-PLAY EXERCISE 7

You are the Customer Service Manager at a fictitious retail centre. A customer wants to see you in order to make a complaint. He has been informed that he is not permitted to smoke in the shopping centre. A security guard approached him whilst he was smoking in the shopping mall area and ordered him to stop smoking. He informs you that the security guard was both confrontational and verbally aggressive in his approach. He wants to know what you intend to do about it.

HOW TO PREPARE AND POSSIBLE ACTIONS

- There are two elements to this situation. The first element is the smoking issue. The customer is not permitted to smoke in the centre as per the information provided within the Westshire Centre pack. You must inform the customer that he is not permitted to smoke within the centre in line with current legislation and company policy. I recommend you inform the customer of this fact in a polite yet resilient manner.

- The second element of the scenario is the complaint that relates to how the security guard has allegedly handled the situation. You will need to apologise for their behaviour and also gather sufficient information in order to carry out an investigation.

- Be prepared for the role actor being confrontational. Remain calm throughout the role play scenario and do not become confrontational or aggressive yourself. Use effective listening skills and open body language at all times.

I have now provided a sample response to this exercise. Read it before using the box on the following page to take notes on how you would deal with this situation.

SAMPLE RESPONSES AND ACTIONS TO EXERCISE 7

"Hello sir, my name is Richard and I am the customer services officer for the centre, thank you for coming to see me today. Please would you explain what the problem is?"

Let the customer speak and listen intently. If they become verbally aggressive, use inappropriate language or confrontational then you must inform them in a clam manner that this kind of behaviour will not be tolerated.

"I am here to help you sir but I must ask you to refrain from using that kind of language. Please remain calm and I will listen to your complaint and try to resolve it to your satisfaction."

As soon as you have listened to the customer's complaint you should first reiterate that smoking is not permitted within the centre. Once you have informed him of this you should apologise for security guards alleged behaviour before gathering sufficient information to deal with that particular element of the complaint.

"OK sir, thank you for providing me with the information. I can confirm that customers are unfortunately not permitted to smoke within the centre. This is to ensure the comfort of our guests and the policy is also in line with UK legislation. However, you are more than welcome to smoke at the designated smoking areas which we have provided for our customers. I am more than happy to inform you exactly where these areas are. In relation to the actions by the security guard, I would like to explore this further. If the security guard has acted in an inappropriate manner I would like to apologise unreservedly. I can assure you that I will personally carry out a full investigation once I have gathered the facts. Can you tell me exactly what he said, where the incident occurred and provide me with a description of the security guard please."

Whilst the customer is providing the information you should listen carefully and demonstrate effective listening skills.

"OK sir, thank you for providing me with the information. I will now carry out a full investigation and speak personally to the security guard. I will contact you as soon as possible to inform you of the outcome of my investigation. Once again I apologise if any offence has been caused and I assure you that this is not the way in which we want to treat our value customers. Is there anything else I can help with you?"

NOTES FOR SAMPLE ROLE-PLAY EXERCISE 7

SAMPLE ROLE-PLAY EXERCISE 8

SAMPLE ROLE-PLAY EXERCISE 8

You are the Customer Service Manager at a fictitious retail centre. A member of staff has been laughing and making fun of one of the other members of staff who has a disability. He has been calling him names and tampering with his wheelchair. The victim has made a complaint and it is your responsibility to speak to the member of staff and take appropriate action.

HOW TO PREPARE AND POSSIBLE ACTIONS

This type of scenario is designed to assess your assertiveness and your ability to stop behaviour that is inappropriate. It is imperative that behaviour of this nature is stopped immediately. It is also important that you explore and clarify in order to ascertain the facts of the incidents and also why the person is behaving as they are.

Don't forget to concentrate on the core competencies at all times during the role-play scenario.

SAMPLE RESPONSES AND ACTIONS TO EXERCISE 8

"Hi, thanks for coming to see me today. I've been made aware of recent incidents that involve you making fun of another member of staff who has a disability. Please can you tell me what has happened?"

The role actor will start to explain his version of events and what has happened. The role actor explains that it was all just a bit of fun and that the person in the wheelchair likes it because it makes him the centre of attention. He says that no harm is intended and it's all a good laugh. If you ask him to stop doing it then he believes it will affect team morale.

Once you have 'explored' a little further, you decide to say:

"Whilst I appreciate morale in the office is important, it is not at the expense of others' misfortune. Even though the person might appear to like it, it can have devastating effects on how they feel and perform at work. This kind of behaviour is not tolerated and due to the severity of it I am going to place you on a warning. Do you understand?"

The role actor now starts to disagree with you, swearing and being verbally abusive in the process. It is important at this stage that you stay calm, maintain an open body stance and stand firm by your decision.

"That kind of language is not tolerated so please do not use it. It is important that you understand fully the implications of your actions towards other people and I stand by my decision to place you on a warning. I do not want to see this kind of behaviour again and will be monitoring the situation in the future."

TIPS FOR HANDLING THE SITUATION

- Any form of bullying or harassment must be dealt with effectively. Do not let it pass by or ignore it. If the role actor tries to persuade you otherwise, you must stand firm.

- Stay calm during the scenario and always remain in control.

- If the role actor starts to swear or uses inappropriate language then you will need to challenge it calmly and assertively.

- In the above example, I have placed the role actor on a warning. Is this essential? You will need to judge each case as it happens but I believe in this case it is important to demonstrate assertiveness and that you have the ability to challenge bullying and harassment effectively. Remember that one of the core competencies is that of respect for race and diversity. This is a diversity issue that needs to be tackled and not ignored.

NOTES FOR SAMPLE ROLE-PLAY EXERCISE 8

SAMPLE ROLE-PLAY EXERCISE 9

SAMPLE ROLE-PLAY EXERCISE 9

You are the manager at a fictitious retail centre. A member of your staff (the role-play actor) approaches you and tells you that another member of staff has been making racist comments about her. She is feeling very upset about the situation and feels threatened by the alleged abuse. She would like to make a complaint.

HOW TO PREPARE AND POSSIBLE ACTIONS

To begin with you need to read the briefing pack. What does it tell you about the scenario and are there any clues that dictate how you should respond to the situation? Remember to look at the six core behavioural skills that you are being assessed against. In this instance you will certainly need to demonstrate 'non-verbal listening' skills. This can be done by utilising effective body language and facial expressions. The person has clearly had a terrible experience and you need to reflect this in your response.

As a police officer you will be required to deal with situations like this. It is important to treat it seriously, take notes relevant to the facts and deal with it quickly and appropriately. Remember to respect diversity at all times.

Once you have listened to what the role actor is saying, you will need to ask probing questions 'exploring and clarifying' exactly what has happened before you make a judgement.

Now take a look at the following sample response to this role-play scenario.

SAMPLE RESPONSES AND ACTIONS TO EXERCISE 9

"Hello, thank you for coming to see me today. I understand you've had a bad experience? I'd like to explore what has happened. Please can you tell me exactly what has happened to you?"

Listen very carefully to what is being and show that you are listening, both verbally and non-verbally. Don't forget to use facial expressions to demonstrate that you are listening effectively. Nod your head and confirm that you understand what is being said. Just by saying "That must have been terrible for you", you are demonstrating the core skill of 'showing understanding'.

"That must have been terrible for you, are you okay for me to ask you some questions about the situation? If at any time you feel uncomfortable please stop me and we will take a break."

"What did the person say to you?"

"When and where did this happen?"

"How did that make you feel?"

"Have they said anything like this to you before?"

"Are you aware of anybody else receiving the same treatment?"

Once you have gathered these initial facts you will need to clarify what has happened. I suggest you use the word 'clarify' when interacting with the role actor. This will demonstrate to the assessors that you are meeting the assessable competency of problem solving.

"OK, before I make any decisions I'd like to clarify exactly what has happened. You say that you have been bullied for a few weeks now and that it is the same person?"

Once you have gathered the facts of the incident it is important to state that this kind of behaviour is not tolerated and that it will be dealt with effectively. Remember that one of the core behavioural skills is 'respect for race and diversity'.

NOTES FOR SAMPLE ROLE-PLAY EXERCISE 9

ADDITIONAL NOTES AND GUIDANCE

- Please note that the sample scenarios provided within this guide are examples only and they will not be the ones that you are assessed against during the assessment centre. Whilst some of them may be similar you must treat each case based the information provided and the facts surrounding the scenario. It is not the scenario that is important but how you deal with it.

- Remember, never to get annoyed or show signs of anger during the interactive exercises.

- The members of staff who are carrying out the fictitious roles may try to make the situation difficult to deal with. They may come across in a confrontational manner during the role-play scenarios so be prepared for this. Don't let it put you on the back foot and remember that they are trying to test your ability to diffuse confrontational situations. You must remain in control at all times and treat the role actor in a sensitive and supportive manner.

- Most importantly, make sure you remember to respect equality and diversity at all times. You will be assessed in this area during every scenario.

- Challenge any inappropriate behaviour immediately during the role-play scenarios. Be firm where appropriate but do not become confrontational.

- Use keywords and phrases from the core competencies where possible.

- Finally, remember to be confident and firm whenever required. However, do respect your role as a customer service manager and provide a high level of service.

GOLDEN TIPS

- Always try to deal with the role actor in a sensitive and supportive manner.

- During the role play activity phase ask appropriate questions in order to gather information surrounding the case.

- Once you have gathered your information you must clarify.

- Explain any relevant documentation in your responses. This will gain you higher marks.

- Make sensible suggestions on how you think you can improve the situation.

- Always interact with the role play actor in a clear and constructive manner.

- Be sure to deal with the issues directly in accordance with the Welcome Pack and any other documentation provided.

Attend a 1-Day intensive Police Officer training course run by former serving Police Officers.

Visit the following website for more details:

www.PoliceCourse.co.uk

how2become

Visit www.how2become.co.uk to find more titles and courses that will help you to pass the police officer selection process:

- Online police officer testing

- 1 Day police officer training course

- Police officer books and DVD's

- Psychometric testing books and CDs.

www.how2become.co.uk